RSA:NC

RSA NEW CONTEMPORARIES
14 - 25 FEBRUARY 2009

The Royal Scottish Academy has a proud tradition of promoting excellence in contemporary art in Scotland. Led by eminent artists and architects it supports the creation, understanding and enjoyment of the visual arts through exhibitions, artist opportunities and related educational talks and events. Re-establishing itself as a leading organisation for the visual arts in Scotland, it has successfully garnered a reputation for the strength of its engaging and diverse exhibitions and the fantastic opportunities it offers both established and emerging artists.

Published for the exhibition at
The Royal Scottish Academy of Art & Architecture
The Mound, Edinburgh, Scotland, EH2 2EL
www.royalscottishacademy.org

CONTE

In an extract from a manuscript in the collection of the Royal Scottish Academy, *Reminiscences of Samuel Mackenzie RSA,* Mackenzie's son has written "In my father's studio at number nineteen (Castle Street, Edinburgh) most of the preliminary or consultation meetings as to the forming of the Royal Scottish Academy were held". In contemporary terms this was a conversation about the formation of a collective, a guild of artists coming together to support and promote their fellow artists. At the heart of these conversations would have been practical ideas for supporting emerging artists. Esme Gordon writing in 1976 states "The Academy devotes one third of its free annual income to educational purposes, maintaining a system of scholarships, prizes and competitions for students." These statements confirm that the Academy has from its beginnings to the present day pursued an active policy of supporting Scottish artists at the start of their professional careers.

Sir Robin Philipson established the Students Open Exhibition over thirty years ago at a time when there were limited opportunities for emerging artists to exhibit their work in city centre galleries. These exhibitions gave students the opportunity to show their work alongside fellow students from other colleges and see their work in a new context in one of the most prestigious exhibiting spaces in Scotland. As an artist led collective the Academy is in a state of constant change, each generation of members contributing to new developments.

The former student open show was very successful for many years, but with numbers increasing and the changing nature of art practice, it had became a victim perhaps of this success. This year for the first time the selection of work was made by Academicians in partnership with the staff of the colleges and we are grateful to them for their advice and guidance. In the words of the programme director, "This will be a show case of painting, sculpture, film-making, photography, printmaking, architecture and installation from the cream of Scotland's emerging artists".

As convener I am grateful to the Staff of the RSA and to the members of the Academy who have given their time and energy over the past year to make this exhibition a success, and to assist the Academy in forging a relationship with artists and architects at the start of their careers. We hope that this relationship will continue as their practice develops.

Professor Will Maclean RSA
Exhibition Convenor
RSA New Contemporaries

ARTIS

Ivonne Adel-Bureos
Sean Ambrose
Ruth Barry
Fiona Beveridge
Jeremy Bidgood
Charlie Billingham
Robert Black
Ross Brown
Louise Brunjes
Darren Buchan
Callum Chapman
Ella Clogstoun
Nick Crawford
Tielia Dellanzo
Grazyna Dobrzelecka
Cornelius Dupre
Greg Fraser
Alastair Frazer
Mary Freeman
Caroline Gallagher
Scott Gordon
Fraser Gray
Kevin Harman
Steven Helm
Rosie Hughes-Jones
Sarah Ingersoll
Katherine Ive
Tor Jonsson
Ai Kato

Silja Leifsdottir
Margaret Livingstone
Stuart Lorimer
Wendy MacDonald
Amelia Martin
Steven J May
Stuart McAdam
Alexander McAndrew
John McLaren
Michail Mersinis
Jane Mulvey
Ashley Nieuwenhuizen
Michael Owen
Ross Perkin
Georgina Porteous
Mary Ramsden
Daisy Richardson
Gemma Saville
Teresa Sciberras
Helen Shaddock
Aisling Shannon
Bridget Steed
Stephanie Straine
Camilla Symons
Euan Taylor
Robin Thomson
Rosie Walters
Ric Warren
Rebecca Witko
Julie Wyness

IVONNE ADEL-BUREOS

GRADUATED: GRAY'S SCHOOL OF ART
eyeandpie@yahoo.co.uk

Ivonne is a graduate of Grays School of Art, Aberdeen where she studied printmaking. She constantly explores ideas in print, breaking boundaries and working with a very reactionary work ethic. She has lived, studied and worked in various locations in the UK, Europe and the USA developing a very urban style dealing mainly with themes of consumerism and recycling - elevating the ordinary. She is continuously bringing together fine art and design and has settled on an understanding that everything comes together in the final composition.

To Ivonne the answer is : live - find - recycle - create.

Images from top:
Her Contemporary Life (detail) [2008]
Fill it to the Top [2008]

SEAN AMBROSE

GRADUATED: GRAY'S SCHOOL OF ART

SN.Ambrose@googlemail.com

I am interested in all architectural forms, but at present my focus is on industrial structures. I am looking at the modern day industrial landscape, but at the same time trying to capture a feeling of nostalgia. I hope to achieve a sense of balance and stillness through the use of colour and tone, which have become fundamentally important in the work. Through my encounters with industrial shape and form I have endeavoured to understand and interpret the mood, presence and space of the industrial environment.

Images from top:
Cable Layers II [2008]
Cable Layers I [2008]

9

RUTH BARRY

GRADUATED: EDINBURGH COLLEGE OF ART
http://ruthbarry.blogspot.com/

With a focus on the premise of experience, I create ambiguous dialogues between fragmented elements to explore understanding and interpretation. Using both found and personal images as starting points, simple drawings and sculptures are activated through performative gestures, highlighting the experiential qualities inherent to the process of making and the occupation of space.

With (often personal) human experience forming a central core of my practice, I shift the parameters of figurative representation, manipulating the image of identity so as to maintain openness as to whom the experience belongs. By utilising an installation based format, drawing, sculpture, photographic and often filmic elements, begin to converse and form relationships with one another, bridging the gap between what is real and what is imagined, and involving the viewer experientially as they navigate their own interpretation and understanding.

Images from top:
Untitled (Rockette) [2009]

FIONA BEVERIDGE

GRADUATED: STRATHCLYDE UNIVERSITY

www.fionabeveridge.co.uk

The Islands That Roof The World : A proposal to re-establish a Scottish slate industry on the west coast of Scotland.

Scottish slate is an invaluable resource. As stocks of reclaimed slate decrease, the distinctive characteristics of our indigenous buildings are being lost. The re-establishment of a slate quarrying industry in Scotland would be of significant value, economically and socially reinvigorating rural communities.

Focused on a coastal village on Luing, this project presents Cullipool as the starting point for the development of a boat based quarrying strategy. Developed using a series of stop motion animation techniques, the architectural proposal presents the development of a harbour and slate processing plant. The detailed scheme sits within an outline proposal of further industrial and social developments on Luing and the overall extraction of slate seams throughout the west coast of Scotland.

Rethinking traditional quarrying typologies, the industrial spaces are immediately rooted in the landscape, carved from the seams which are processed within them. The temporary nature of the industrial spaces and investment of the slate waste in community projects aim to present a scheme which is sensitive to the fragile landscape on which the industry relies.

Images from top:
Imagining the New Harbour [2008]
Inside a Processing Bay [2008]

JEREMY BIDGOOD

GRADUATED: EDINBURGH COLLEGE OF ART
www.jeremybidgood.com

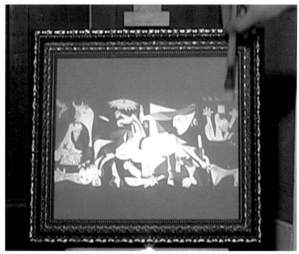

Jeremy Bidgood's practice largely involves installed films, animations and performances. Alongside his work as an artist he is an accomplished puppeteer and theatre director, and recipient of the RSC Buzz Goodbody Directing Award.

Belief, ritual, and the performative function of the art object and viewer dominate my practice. The rituals of religion and the art world are often not far apart. Ritual is the most obvious effect the divine has on the world - it is a physical enunciation of something otherwise difficult/impossible to see or experience. In the same way the performative happenings that take place around a work of art (travelling to the gallery, queuing, buying tickets, and giving donations) are often more meaningful and important that the art object itself. These rituals are an 'Aura Machine'. They imbue the art-work with the sanctity it so easily loses as it is whored across the world on postcards, key-rings and rubbers. This is not the same Aura that Walter Benjamin described. Instead it is an Aura of fashion and semantics, created by the rituals of the art-world rather than visual scarcity. It is an Aura that uses the souvenir rubber like the religious icon to further its impact whilst placing a primacy on the act of visiting the gallery. There is no demand for lengthy worship, just the visit and the necessary accompanying rituals. Rituals that make the viewer a performer in the pay of Art.

I explore these incidental performances through large scale projected installations, performances and short films. I seek to make the viewer implicit in my work: part of a mechanised performance reflecting the mechanisation of repeated, often unconsidered, ritual.

Images from top:
Art Attack (Performance) [2008]
Art Machine: Good Art Can Take A Long Time [2008]

CHARLIE BILLINGHAM

GRADUATED: EDINBURGH COLLEGE OF ART

www.charliebillingham.com

Through referencing and appropriating celebrated aspects of art history I intend to create complex visual narratives, which explore the tension between humour and a variety of more serious and poignant subjects. In my most recent work I have been looking at two of Seurat's most famous works, 'Bather's at Asnières' (1884) and 'Sunday afternoon on the island of La Grande Jatte' (1884-1886). Although the original paintings work as a pair, raising a number of serious socio-political issues, they can only be seen together in print, since the former is in London and the latter in Chicago. I have played with this idea by recreating the paintings full size in an exaggerated half-tone style. This technique is not only a cheeky reference to pointillism, but also to printed images and image reproduction. The resultant lack of detail from this translation is evocative of the loss of information from not being able to see the two original works together.

Other sources I have used for my work in the past include: Warhol's Elvis paintings, Malevich's Black Square and the history of monochrome abstraction. As well as art historically referenced work, I have also used sweet wrappers, balloons, cartoons and clouds as inspiration. An aspect which links most of my work is that I use traditional art production methods to illustrate light-hearted conceptual ideas in visually exciting ways.

Images from top:
Bathers at Asnièrs [2008/09]
A Sunday Afternoon on the Island of La Grande Jatte [2008/09]

ROBERT BLACK

GRADUATED: GLASGOW SCHOOL OF ART
rabphotos@btinternet.com

Madonna: These images reflect a woman, a mother and a wife, as well as someone who is a lover. The child on the right hand side reflects uncertainty, a change in social standing and jealousy towards a newborn child. It is a reflection of life in its purest form – the innocence of a child. The woman reflects realistically a mother as well as a wife in much the way that most do and not in a supernatural way, someone who women can relate to and in fact live up to.

For Pete's Sake: This work stems from a lack of understanding, a need for some knowledge of people with a less fortunate lifestyle and future, people with a void in their lives, people who carry excess baggage – baggage they would much rather forget, from alcoholism to drug, physical and emotional abuse. The coherent lack of education for one reason or another is evident in the lifestyle choices that some have made.

I wanted to obtain an understanding as well as to be able to show some consideration for their misfortune. I used my camera as a tool to gain access to their world and then used the images as a dialogue of reason and a voice in the white space between myself and the subject, a view of emotions in a part of society that would normally be overlooked. It is designed to make the viewer look more in to its content rather than just look and pass it by.

Images clockwise from top:
For Pete's Sake I, II & III (From series of 13 prints) [2008]
Madonna (from series of 3 prints) [2008]

14

ROSS BROWN

GRADUATED: DUNCAN OF JORDANSTONE COLLEGE OF ART

bawbegcrew@hotmail.com

There is a gulf between the Utopian vision on the architect's drawing board and the fragile reality of real space. This divide is bridged through building, in its most primary form the creation of the dwelling. Interior and exterior are established through construction; within and without, self and other.

"As Heidegger explained; one's capacity to live on this earth – to 'dwell' in the phenomenological sense – is an essentially architectural experience. The very Being of being is linked to one's situatedness in the world."

Establishing "situatedness" within the ever changing modern built environment poses difficulty often resulting in feelings of disorientation and dislocation. The wastelands and their abandoned structures are unstable environments; an interim space between architecture and nature. As such, the wasteland is used within my work as a vehicle reflecting the difficulty associated with establishing a sense of place within a landscape that is in a constant state of flux.

My most recent paintings feature architecture within states of both construction and ruin. This interplay of chaos and order is reflected in the painting process employed as drips and abstract elements distort the foundations of the image and play with the idea of "surface". Influences on my work include the writings of Gaston Bachelard and the films of the Russian director Andrei Tarkovsky.

Images from top:
Wasteland Double [2008]
Within the Ruins of the Present [2008]

15

LOUISE BRUNJES

GRADUATED: GLASGOW SCHOOL OF ART
www.louisebrunjes.co.uk

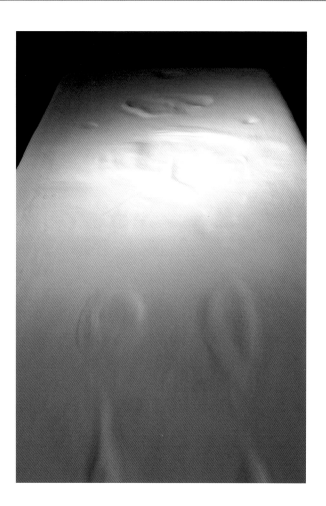

I recall the way we were touched
Cooling in the present and warming up the past

It's the difference between an object that holds memory in a tactile way (a bed whose sheets still hold a shape and smell, fingerprints on a recently emptied glass), and a document that reminds us of that which is gone; that which we are no longer able to touch, (a photo of your old house, a video of a child, or a record that will forever play sounds that belong in the past)

The objects permeate the ephemeral imprints of everyday touches, suspending the aging process of that object in a way that a photo never could, so palpably physical are the materials. Using plaster, latex and wax, the aging process is frozen, making it clean and still, but ever immediate and tactile.

Forever in context, they live a solid life.

This is a practice based on touch and piecing together a history, a narrative, by reading the physical memory that we carry around etched on our skin. It's these ingrained details that are our present, but provide the key to understanding our past. But how can we look at the body and its immediacy in a tactile way using such dry, detached, time based media?

Like dust, like fog, like clouds of memory.

Be Not Another [2008]

DARREN BUCHAN

GRADUATED: EDINBURGH COLLEGE OF ART
www.darrenbuchanart.com

As humans, we sometimes feel the need to escape our urban environments and expose ourselves to the elements of nature. My work is inspired by nature and the various landscapes that I have discovered through interactions from walking & camping.

The main focus of my work is based on surfaces and texture, and the creation of contrasting and structural shapes. The processes involved in making my work are physical and raw in nature.

At present I am focused on the idea of a designed landscape, a fabrication domesticated from human presence and agricultural interference. I want to create the idea of a structural and ordered environment with various divisions and boundaries similar in nature to a patch/grid format much like our cities and towns.

My work is derived from personal experiences taken from my various travels around Scotland and has led to an intuitive way of working.

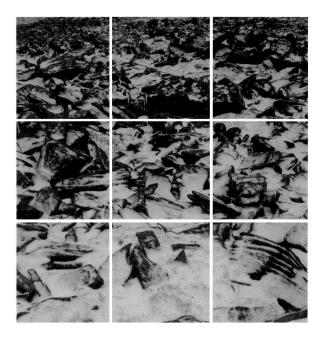

Stuc a' chroin [2008]

CALLUM CHAPMAN

GRADUATED: GRAY'S SCHOOL OF ART
no_pocket_for_kitty@hotmail.com

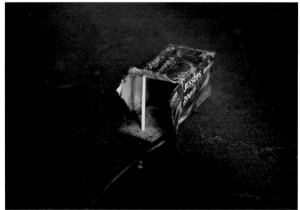

My work past and present has consisted working mainly with the photographic medium as a tool to document fabricated situations that are real or imagined. I find endless fun in rearranging the world around me by making little interventions that I would describe as having an almost theatrical narrative. I would define my work as an exploration into themes such as interaction and anti interaction within the context of everyday ordinary spaces.

My current work has been constructed by exploring such interweaving themes. Firstly I am constructing and exploring intimate spaces by using themes such as concealment, confinement and traps. This has led me to continue an ongoing journey to fabricate everyday objects and scenes from domestic life which are then made extraordinary by either intervention or by being photographed. These fabrications relate to both myself, the house, and the operations of a camera. Traps of vision and intimacy invite the viewer to create imaginative poetic sensual possibilities or act as triggers of security and unease, while images of cloth and sheets provoke traces of a journey of the unconscious. They are temporary shelters for daydreams that reminisce child-like constructions to create imaginary drama in a playful state of flux. But perhaps most importantly they are little windows to a witness of intimacy that invite and lure the viewer to gaze into their daily world around them in new ways.

Images from top:
Untitled I [2008/09]
Untitled II [2008/09]

ELLA CLOGSTOUN

GRADUATED: GLASGOW SCHOOL OF ART

ellacello@yahoo.it

I am interested in the similarities between recent consumer culture and a Catholic tradition, both of which require an immediacy in response; which is achieved through an overload of aesthetic information. I utilise cheap and mass-produced objects, in the manner of the overtly-decadent aesthetic, which emanates from religious traditions.

My fascination with the Kitsch and devotional Catholic faith has grown from anthropological observation. In particular, I have drawn conclusions from the Romani culture in Eastern Europe and semi-indigenous tribes of Mexico who have been given the expression 'Rascuachismo' by high Mexican society in order to distance itself from a perceived cheap and lowborn culture. It could be argued that both of these ethnic minorities have embraced a Catholic faith in order to be accepted by wider society. The decadence of Catholic modes of expression finds a convenient analogue in plastic totems of a westernised consumer culture.

In my work, I aim to blend the disparate elements of mass-production within consumerist society and those of the labour-intensive, hand-to-mouth lifestyle.

The Kitsch carries in its wake the contradictory. My deployment of its methods doesn't attempt to reiterate these issues. Instead, I draw attention to, and play with the tension created between primitive imagery and formal modernity, and the acceptance of folk traditions within a "high art" framework. I attempt to fuse together the oppositional and create a hybrid aesthetic which encompasses these concerns.

Untitled I, II, III [2008]

NICK CRAWFORD

GRADUATED: MACKINTOSH SCHOOL OF ARCHITECTURE

nickcrawford@dixonjones.co.uk

The seaplane has made a return to Glasgow after more than 50 years with the first service in Europe to operate from a city centre, linking to towns and islands on the west coast. This project proposes a move downstream from Pacific Quay to Central Station, and an increase in flight frequency and destinations.

It considers the potential for a sustainable and integrated transport system within today's compact city, proposing seaplanes, which require limited infrastructure and have the potential to be located in the heart of any city containing an expanse of water. Situated on the Clyde at one of the key crossing points, the building heightens the intensity of traffic marking the intersection of the river, rail and road arteries, offering multiple opportunities for travellers, passers by and tourists alike. The project includes a 100 room 5-star hotel in order to maximise the site's unique location.

The building, given its unique location on the Clyde, is driven by unique structural and environmental parameters as well as its symbolic significance as a 'gateway' to the city.

Existing granite piers are used to support a new linking footbridge which spans across the river and passes beneath the hotel tower allowing views up into the full-height atrium. The tower considers what density of development the river's edge demands and can sustain, while providing the opportunity of dramatic views along the river, to the sea beyond and the spectacle of the seaplanes and their flight paths. The footbridge continues down to the terminal platforms, which unfold beneath the bridge towards the water, always allowing passengers and passers-by to see the planes coming and going beneath the bridges and along the water.

Image from top:
Glasgow Seaplane Terminal (Sectional Perspective) [2008]
Glasgow Seaplane Terminal (Sectional Perspective Detail) [2008]

TIELIA DELLANZO

GRADUATED: DUNCAN OF JORDANSTONE COLLEGE OF ART

dlanzo@blueyonder.co.uk

My practice is led through the observations and investigations of public spaces and thresholds, both psychological and physical. How we occupy spaces and the liminal actions that are emitted in conjunction with the space that we co-habit are central concerns in my work.

My goal is to develop inventive works that focus on the public and spatial foundations of the civic realm. My philosophical practice is driven by an ambition to fulfil the potential pleasures that exist at the liminal threshold between the lived and the built. This creative process is underpinned by a capacity to create valuable relationships that uncover and value the desires and experience of a variety of patrons. Access is understood not as a dispensation but as the magnificent model; creating spaces that have a rendering of experience for all who engage in the choreography of actions, physically and conceptually, arousing a sense of ownership through occupation. My professional practice in fine art; installation art; 3d objects; specialist glass practice and philosophy focuses on the realm of public space.

This installation has been developed using the above practices merged with historical and cultural research.

Mirror Corridor [2008]

GRAZYNA DOBRZELECKA

GRADUATED: EDINBURGH COLLEGE OF ART
grazyna.dobrzelecka@googlemail.com

I'm interested in those details of the surroundings which are generally disregarded. Things that are nothing special in themselves and yet crucial for us.

Printmaking process holds some fascinating factors for me. The process of repetition that becomes a pattern for every day activity on one hand. I'm yet again turning the wheel of the printing press and another print becomes another step, turning another page of the book, wakening up in the morning. Each one is the same and yet different and one might (or might not) take an unexpected shift or result.

Imprint becomes a moment in time on the other hand. Every place and object holds a history. All the scratches, dirt and imperfections have a story to tell. Envisioning the marks enables to mark the presence and the trace once left behind.

Contradiction has been a vivid part of my work for a while. That is in terms of juxtaposing materials that normally don't meet each other; in arranging a dead straight line and an organic curve; in confronting technique and the idea.

Works of Rachel Whiteread, Piotr C. Kowalski and Lucy Skaer have a great impact on my practice. Capturing the ghost of something that was or is, through distilling surroundings.

Movies by Jim Jarmusch and Krzysztof Kieslowski influenced my studio practice as well. Especially the characteristic structure. In several cases the movie consists of individual stories. Although independent, the stories interact. People and events penetrate each other's spaces and only a careful viewer is able to detect them. Accordingly, I like to build up my work in series. This approach relates also to a journey.

A physical journey, a journey in time and a wondering eye of the viewer have been significant. The recent works balance between portraiture, narration and abstraction.

STRONGBOX [2008]

CORNELIUS DUPRE
GRADUATED: EDINBURGH COLLEGE OF ART
acjdupre@hotmail.com

I work with many different approaches and materials. I like to work small and fast as well as big and slow. I'm interested in the meaning and history of things, and use both found objects and raw materials in my practice. Work starts with a vision and then goes through various stages of development until a satisfactory resolution is reached. I try to maintain a balance between intuitive action and planned construction. I make objects, images, events and videos; I like to make work both outside and inside the gallery. Some of my work is long lasting, made from concrete or metal and some is completely ephemeral, lasting only for a few hours or a day. I often archive my material in the form of books, and I find the books themselves a new form of work. Art historical influences include land art and formalism and influences from outside the world of art include ancient cultures and physical phenomena. The work presented for the RSA New Contemporaries is entitled 'Prop', and deals with the way I feel art is perceived. I personally veer between a respect for skill and tradition and a lust for new approaches and ideas.

Growth [2008]
Pipette [2008]

GREG FRASER

GRADUATED: GLASGOW SCHOOL OF ART
www.gregfraserart.com

The process of creating a work and the interactive processes inherent within this is what drives my studio practice. By combining a deeply intuitive approach with studious decision making I hope to generate an emotive response in the viewer. My process is anchored by introspective motivations and a desire to explore my own personal history. I aim to communicate this to the spectator through the form and content of my work; a purely visual language.

The visual sources I use to create my work are taken from hidden urban spaces such as the deserted archaeological remnants of Glasgow's industrial past. I wish to express the sense of history and abandonment of these spaces, as well as to represent the passage of time.

Image from top:
Town Houses [2008]
East End Athanor [2008]
Photography by Ewan Cameron

ALASTAIR FRAZER
GRADUATED: GLASGOW SCHOOL OF ART
www.citycrimeradio.org

I am particularly interested in developing work that describes a 'way of being', and consequently a 'way to'- a pathway embedded with the effects of that transition. The representation of this 'way' in the work is often formed as an expression of a mental passage- possibly seen in the psychological effects of crossing over from one idea or state to another- transcendence, transgression, transference. This thought process is decision making certainly, but more to do with perpetuating multiple ideas about a thing rather than purely seeking sanctuary in a conclusion. To me, the emotional subconscious of desire is a force that is important to relate to and is parallel to the potentially abstract 'dynamic' properties of a physical thing. I find the curious interplay of forces upon one's own senses to be relational to the configurations between material and process found in spaces and in objects, and I therefore see the self and the built environment to be tied in a co-dependent exploration.

In my recent work- as shown here in this exhibition - I have formed an idea of a contemporary archaeology as a way of 're-finding' objects in the present. In what I have termed 'ergonomic archaeology'- I wish to emphasize the tension between the force of velocity and dynamics of form on one hand, and the timeless waiting of the symbols and signs discovered in artefacts. I imagine the gazebo-like structure to be a container or frame, making a 'scene' of potential discovery out of a given site. It offers an archaeologically minded consideration of its contents not as disparate and unrelated events, but belonging to a continuum of origin, drift and exploration. Important to me is the sense that one thing is always 'feeling' for another in a perpetual engagement that is impressionistic, metaphoric and unspoken.

Images from top:
Ergonomic Archaeology [2008]
Untitled (Ergonomic Wheelbarrow) [2008]

MARY FREEMAN

GRADUATED: GRAY'S SCHOOL OF ART

www.maryfreemanart.com

As modern beings we place huge value on our individuality. Yet do we ignore a deeper-rooted cyclical basis of life in the futile pursuit of decorating our existence? Does the ever-changing context of our surroundings conceal an ultimate truth?

The notion of "balance" can be applied to most aspects of life. It is impossible to define a positive having not explored its binary negative. Thus even the most seemingly unlinked of ideas, are supported by their inter-dependant rejection of one another. Despite the irony of this, it provides the necessary impetus that cumulates in the continual progression of society.

In a hypermodern world, driven by the greed of market forces and the perceived luxury of choice, it has become increasingly difficult to locate our singularity. How can we express our free will in a world that is dictated by conformity? The fight to develop original thought is futile. It is this futility, balanced by the promise of the future that I aim to expose.

My work aims to engage the viewer directly and challenge them to question their predicament, to contemplate their expectations and to discover the truth of their own existence.

Introspecterior [2008]

There is unease in the drive behind my work, a disquiet born out of city centre living. An aspiration for space, for control over my thoughts, my purchases and my navigation through the city centre area means that I am drawn to elements and objects that are on the periphery of the landscape. I view these objects/materials as happenings that proliferate the landscape as found sculptures, public art works created through subconscious interaction; compositional traces of human activity. I am interested in this act of intuitive decision making and the way that such decisions or accidents can foster new connections between elements. This is how I approach making my sculpture/installation and this process and the materials used are a very important part of my work.

My work often appears temporary and un-fixed; this has been significant in all work, suggesting the latent potential for movement and change.

Previous work has used building materials, as they were regularly encountered in my daily journeys through the city centre. Now working from a home studio, the materials used and scale of work have shifted. Gravity, temporality, structure and volume all still form core elements of the work. The work seeks to be read as abstract form and sits somewhere between the autonomous and the associative.

Multiplex [2008]

27

SCOTT GORDON

GRADUATED: DUNCAN OF JORDANSTONE COLLEGE OF ART

www.loopshaunt.co.uk

Artist. Producer. D J. My work has generally been based around the production of music and video but more recently I have focused mainly on music. I have been making electronic music for roughly seven years, as well as djing locally in Dundee and organising events/nights. I'm currently working on various musical projects including film soundtrack, recording bands and my own music. As well as this I have began teaching digital workshops in Perth working with local kids, teaching music and video production. However as an artist I'm willing to branch out creatively... Or, if you have some money then I'll do pretty much anything you want... If you would like to contact me then I am available through loopshaunt@hotmail.com.

:120

Constructing of three video pieces,120 is an amalgamation of video footage filmed and edited to the tempo of 120bpm. Each fragment of film was captured with a relevance to that tempo, for example a ball bouncing on a piece of glass would be bounced precisely on the beat or an object that was spun or twisted would move starting and finishing on the beat. The outcome is a collection of footage each with the same underlying rhythmical properties that are then orchestrated into a 3 minute video piece. This technique is applied to three video pieces and played as a triptych. It produces a rhythmical visual feast and has an almost hypnotic -mantric appeal. The pieces run continuously syncopating together as a whole.

:120 [2008]

FRASER GRAY

GRADUATED: DUNCAN OF JORDANSTONE COLLEGE OF ART
www.frasergray.com

Fraser Gray works in spray paint, emulsion and oils to create bold imagery exploring our country's colonialism. His works contrast graphic shapes representing consumerist ideals against the nostalgic imagery of traditional landscape and figure painting. By painting and extending the work on the wall, Gray creates a singular context in which they can be viewed, painting large scale installations unique to each exhibit. By producing temporary site specific work, Gray tries to prevent his work from being viewed as an 'object' or a commodity, something he feels could contradict the political narrative found in many of his paintings.

Out with his studio practice, Fraser also works extensively with community projects teaching painting and drawing as well as doing mural commissions internationally in places such as Barcelona and Hong Kong.

Images from top:
Empire (Degree Show) [2008]
Empire (detail) [2008]

KEVIN HARMAN

GRADUATED: EDINBURGH COLLEGE OF ART

www.kevinharman.co.uk

My work deals with the raw strength of objects. The objects I use seem to be extensions of power, instruments that cause impact. I aim to root out the hidden beauty within these items and change how we see them in everyday life. I do this by collecting and using common objects that have a gritty, nostalgic feel. I find it helps to converse with viewers and allows an access point to my work. I decide what will be used to construct a work by putting subject materials in a room and allow them to communicate with one another, then through an instinctive reaction, I put them together the way they tell me to. I feel like the tool that allows these objects to breathe.

My sculptures are made through a compulsive reaction to the familiar. I like to get objects stripped back to their essence, and then use them in an alternative way, but always in keeping with their primary function. When I put the subjects together, it's important that they flow as one piece of work. And it's crucial that each object doesn't lose its functionality as an individual entity. Most people know what the objects I choose are and this helps to converse and develop their own interpretation of what's happening in my work.

By its nature, my practice involves creating temporary sculptures with hints of performance and important elements of recycling in our current climate. My work reconfigures everyday objects and through my working process, it allows people to see what's already there in a different light; it surfaces the objects' unseen raw beauty.

Love Thy Neighbour [2008]

STEVEN HELM

GRADUATED: GLASGOW SCHOOL OF ART
stevenmhelm@googlemail.com

At this stage I believe that I am building upon a mode of inquiry into how I take responsibility for practicing as an artist. I have come to realise that Art, for me, represents a resistance to economic, cultural, social and religious facts and that being an artist involves taking responsibility for a kind of disobedience when producing artwork both publicly and privately. My intention as an artist is to let go of the notion of outcome and possession and to commit myself to forms of action that lend themselves to surrender, presence, and latent excess.

I attempt to use sculpture and installations as platforms or vessels that attests to these headless forms of action, that attend the hand, and also become tools for engaging with and emancipating myself from facts. I use wood and metal to try and compose formal structures and shapes that are designed for the display and/or to facilitate actions involving base or excess materials such as clay and soil.

Over the last year my work has been informed by George Bataille's theory of l'informe (the formless), In which he spoke of the tasks of words instead of their meaning and required that each thing have its own form and that what formless designates "has no rights in any sense, and gets itself squashed everywhere, like a spider or an earthworm." This began to trigger a shift towards, what Bataille termed, a 'heterological' approach to making work, which is, in essence, the science of what is entirely 'other'.

Images from top:
Heedless [2008]
Heedless (detail) [2008]

31

ROSIE HUGHES-JONES

GRADUATED: GLASGOW SCHOOL OF ART

rhughesjones@yahoo.co.uk

My experience growing up in a very rural environment and moving to the city is often the stimulus for my work, and through materials, process and architectural spaces I try to suggest a general balance between rural and urban, while at the same time, attempting to trigger a more individual response and evoke a sense of the feeling self; an awareness of bodily presence and experience through smell, materials and scale.

The process involved in making is integral to my practice, and is implied by the traces of activity that are left and the alterations to materials that I make. This references themes of domesticity and traditional labour and craft activities that are present in my work. The integrity to materials and the level of finish is focussed and vital to the works' reading.

The context for my work is important. I focus on the structure of the room and the source of natural light in a space, introducing the outside to the inside. I add a suggestion of taste, touch and smell; letting the work function on an instinctive, bodily level. I often use natural materials that are used for survival; they protect, preserve and nourish such as beeswax, silk, fur and honey. Within the context in which I present them, their function in nature is redundant and the materials become seductive and are used to trigger something visceral in the viewer.

Swarm Migration [2008]

SARAH INGERSOLL

GRADUATED: GLASGOW SCHOOL OF ART

sarah@dwarfbaby.org

My work stems from a kind of personal mythology created to understand and order elements within the past and present mediation of experience. I am intrigued by the comedy and tragedy inherent in our attempt to balance and rationalise existence as we find it. I am interested in the tales we tell ourselves, the ones we make up as we go along and those told to us from childhood, tales supposed to explain how we got from there to here, but which remain fictions.

While my themes tend toward the bleak and sometimes threatening, I cannot help but look to the lighter, more humorous side and try to interject this as much as possible into what I do. Transformation, mortality, history, and the meeting of fact and fantasy are recurring subjects within my work, often taking the form of staged photography, collage, and sculptures. The sometime use of animal as metaphor within my work is a natural device to gain the distance at times needed for this exploration, while the use of friends and family as models and participants reaffirms an intimacy.

I am trying to create new worlds in which to reflect elements of this one. At its simplest, art is a conduit for what we think to be inexpressible and the act of making an affirmation of the search for firmer ground.

Something About the Days Getting Shorter [2008]

KATE IVE

GRADUATED: EDINBURGH COLLEGE OF ART

www.kate-ive.co.uk

It's not about knowledge. It is not about answers. It's not about technology. It's not about right and it's not about wrong. Sometimes it's not even about us. It's a bit about balance. Sometimes it's about questioning but it's not always about solutions...

My work benefits from many varied influences and is heavily research based. It is frequently constructed from a combination of elements and installations, with the emphasis on how they influence one another and us. In many ways, this relates to 'connectivity'. In today's culture of striving for faster accessibility, this is a pertinent area for exploration. The way in which we connect with ourselves, each other, and position ourselves within the ebb and flow of our surroundings, informs my approach.

In addition to 'connectivity', one area of my research that combines all these concepts is an investigation into skin (both literally and symbolically) and skin-like coverings; be they protective, illusionary or misleading. This in turn leads to questions of possible changes in perspective, bringing me to examine ideas of authenticity.

A large part of my approach and exploration is through construction; interlinking raw and delicate elements. The action of looking is key and the connection between looking and seeing is equally important. These techniques allow the development of powerful yet subtle dialogues in my installations, drawings and photography.

It's not about here. It's not about there. It's not about then and it's not about now. Mostly, it's about stopping and equally about looking and listening. It's about making the connection.

If Walls Could Talk (Interior) [2008]

TOR JONSSON
GRADUATED: GLASGOW SCHOOL OF ART
torjonsson@me.com

This work explores ontological imaginations through which immediate surroundings are filtered and understood. A narrative is formed within these constructed landscapes - 'upward into the depths'.

My images aspire to convey a feeling of something beyond appearances, because people, ideas and the places where they live, the traces they leave are always something more, something deeper. Beauty and light, the poetic and the absurd are some of the themes I am drawn towards.

In the working process I try to show what things can be. Inspiration and research matures into concept and theory that can be utilised in an intuitive fashion. I often fall in love with an idea, a gut-feeling - the gap between one thought and the next.

Event Horizon [2008]

AI KATO

GRADUATED: DUNCAN OF JORDANSTONE COLLEGE OF ART
tinyjap@googlemail.com

Ai Kato (born in Kanazawa, Japan 1986) is a Japanese sculptor, currently living in the U.K. While drawing and printmaking have always been her preferred media in particular, she started experimenting with sculpture in the beginning of 2007. Since then she has been making both two and three dimensional pieces as various forms of expression. Using animal parts and other natural found objects, she crafts a mythology of creatures that sway between the reality and supernatural.

All her works evolve from impulsive line drawings that bare naked emotions. Drawing and engraving are explored as poetry, whereas sculptures focus on the impermanence of life through use of fragile media. Mix of ethos, spontaneity, vulgarity and vulnerability, handled with a drop of humour.

Amok [2008]

SILJA LEIFSDOTTIR

GRADUATED: GLASGOW SCHOOL OF ART
www.siljaleifsdottir.com

We all manoeuvre ourselves through life with the help of rational and emotional decisions, trying to find a meaning. But sometimes what you find is not what you were looking for. What do you then choose; the knowledge and the burden that comes with it, or the more blissful ignorance. Or is there a perfect balance of the two?

According to 20th century folklore, the laws of aerodynamics prove that the bumblebee should be incapable of flight, as it does not have the capacity in terms of wing size or beat per second to fly. Not being aware of scientists 'proving' it cannot fly, the bumblebee succeeds under 'the power of its own ignorance'.

It is the absurd beauty in the attempt to control destiny that I find fascinating.

Gravity is a force of nature that is just as inevitable as death.

It is also responsible for keeping the earth and all the other planets in the orbits around the sun. Without it, life as we know it, would not exist.

In spite of this knowledge, mankind have been attempting to conquer this force for centuries, dreaming about weightlessness and the ability to fly. And in a sense we can.

Science might be the pursuit of knowledge, but sometimes it's easier to let go if you forget about gravity.

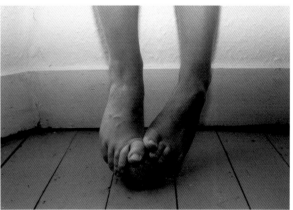

Images from top:
Its easier to let go if you forget about gravity [2008]
On Gravity [2008]

MARGARET LIVINGSTONE

GRADUATED: GRAY'S SCHOOL OF ART

www.artist-at-work.co.uk

"I hate talking about my work. Especially when I am involved in the obsessive panic of making it".

My work is concerned with our interactions with technology and the way the Internet acts as an instant provider of gratification for a whole generation. I use humour and irony to ask questions. I always start with a central idea and a basic structure, but the process of creation introduces its own shifts, tangents, complexities and connections. I wish for clarity; however it's usually a case of clinging on to my initial emotional response to the topic I am exploring. Sometimes it feels like I might drown in the many possible solutions and hope that when I do surface with something that it at the very least reflects my journey. My work is always emotional and is a reflection of my experience which I presume is much the same as anyone else's experience. Significantly it's never quite what I want it to be, there's always something missing, something more to be said – and consequently there is always the need to create something else.

Where the Wild Things Are [2008]

STUART LORIMER

GRADUATED: DUNCAN OF JORDANSTONE COLLEGE OF ART

stuartlorimer@hotmail.co.uk

I make paintings that juxtapose different styles of painting with my own personal iconography. I use magical imagery to explain real experiences and events to create work that has an otherworldly quality.

My influences include classical history painting, the literature of South American Magical Realists, comic book art and contemporary textile design. I often work on a monumental scale where I feel uninhibited and able to produce work that is highly expressive. I have started making small works on board which at first I used as a means of testing ideas and compositions before committing to a larger canvas, however these paintings have now become an integral part of my practice. My paintings are not premeditated and a finished work is the result of a process of constant development and revision.

I synthesise an abstract use of paint and colour with figuration. My recent work falls into two categories. The first, complicated narratives acted out between figures, distorted creatures and areas of abstract paint. My second approach focuses on the urgency and expressive potentialities of paint and the impact of the image. The mood of my paintings can be violent, comic, and lugubrious and at times I use deliberately attractive or ugly subject matter. I have adoration for the lineage of painting history and try to convey this along with contemporary concerns in my art.

New works made possible with financial assistance from the Dundee Visual Artists Award Scheme

Mother of Moonlight [2008]

WENDY MacDONALD

GRADUATED: GRAY'S SCHOOL OF ART
www.wendymacdonald.co.uk

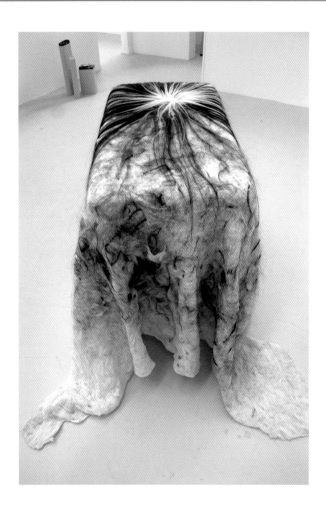

My practice explores the notions surrounding the concept 'Maternal Erasure'. I consider gender deconstruction, questioning efforts to avoid biological essentialism that leave the female pregnant body in limbo. Of interest is the role bio-technology plays in shaping society's view of procreation with current research in human-animal embryology. This research bears a resemblance to eugenic ideology based on the premise of progress for civilisation, which opens many crucial questions for the 21st Century. Is this a transgression of human - animal identity and does it lead to a de-sexualised humanity? What will it mean to be human in the future, if we rely solely on the mechanisms of science for health and procreation? Do we really want to live in a virtual world where machines are more intelligent than humans, where animals and plant life are made artificial by the application of bio-technology? What happens to our innate ability to love and heal, which I believe is much more powerful, if we let ourselves be dominated by the promises of technology? The intention of my practice is to hint to the mysteries of this life, arguing that science and technology will never completely rescue us from our ultimate reality.

Love Renounces its Object [2008]

AMELIA MARTIN

GRADUATED: DUNCAN OF JORDANSTONE COLLEGE OF ART

amelia_byjove@hotmail.com

Born in 1984, Amelia Martin's Highland roots have remained important and have served to form an underlying tone in her art practice combined with experiences and places travelled. Thoughts are continually changing and evolving, still there emerges a thread weaving its way through different ideas. Throughout her work subject matter becomes subsidiary to the compositional elements, exploration of negative spaces, angles and juxtapositions. Adding to this the atmospheric palette choice contributes a subtlety and sensitivity to the paintings.

Tap [2008]

STEVEN JAMES MAY

GRADUATED: UNIVERSITY OF DUNDEE, SCHOOL OF ARCHITECTURE

stevenjmay1976@googlemail.com

An Examination of the Representations of Venice.

In its past reflection there was more life than the world in which it had existed. Venice and its reflections. Reflecting both its physical and metaphysical characteristics in its many representations do we find the actual and virtual representations of an empire lost in time. In almost all portrayals do we find the celebration of the most serene republic.

What is it about Venice that evokes such universal fondness and re-imagination? There is the inherently paradoxical situation in the constant stream of new imagery of this city at the end of its existence; or is it? Do these new representations move the spirit of Venice from its decaying, atrophying physical locale to the common collective consciousness and life eternal? In my thesis work I examined some of the representational methods used and the language of such portrayal, and invest the gleaned knowledge towards an integrated design project.

Venice may not be with us for much longer but as it decays, the nostalgia and regard for things such known and lost continue to enthral and interest the subject of Venice to the world at large. In this spirit of such wistfulness; Venice is Dead. Long live Venice!

Relfections of Venice [2007]

STUART McADAM

GRADUATED: DUNCAN OF JORDANSTONE COLLEGE OF ART

www.stuartmcadam.com

What'll I do? What'll I show you?

I did five a day for a full week. I had brought some things to talk about. But it turned out that the piece was about creating a situation that changed as I engaged with people and that in turn influenced my decisions. I had some sounds playing, a few beers, and some other things I thought I'd need. The opening talk lasted from 7 until 11pm, and we sent out for pizza.

I had a large brush hanging behind the door to the room. In amongst all the noises, someone asked me, "What's the brush for?" and I said, "Sweeping the floor". She laughed, and it created a new environment. I rearranged the room as the week progressed, the sounds changed, new people came and we discussed things as they came up. It was very liberating.

I still don't know the answer, but I was always one for telling stories, and I liked the sound of all those words and sentences, no matter what they meant.

| Loud outcry, clamour, shouting | ...
| Uproar, Brawl | ...
| To pick a quarrel | ...
| Disgust, annoyance, discomfort, (literally seasickness) | ...
| Hurting, injury, damage | ...
| Unpleasant situation | ...
| Ship | ...

The sense of it (the word) is against both suggestions

DIN

Images from top:
Performance @ WASPS Dennistoun, Glasgow [2008]
Nausea (Text piece) [2008]

ALEXANDER McANDREW

GRADUATED: EDINBURGH COLLEGE OF ART

alex.mcandrew@yahoo.co.uk

My work finds joy in all the things that are bad for you. I like mass manufactured plastic materials and dirty jokes. I like shiny glamorous surfaces and objects that are utterly pointless and often inexpertly made. I like to play with scale and make people laugh.

I use humour to disarm the viewer and show the pleasure to be found in artificial materials and sexual content. Often I like my work to seem as if it exists in a different reality, creating a place for strange and unusual things to occur. Also I seek to undermine a lot of the so called seriousness of certain types of art through my work.

Torn Apart [2008]

JOHN McLAREN

GRADUATED: GLASGOW SCHOOL OF ART

okrra@hotmail.com

I spend much of my time travelling, exploring, and experiencing other cultures first hand. I supplement these experiences with secondary research into the histories, religions and cultural practices of the places I visit. Most, if not all of my work is a direct response to this research.

The Golden Horde [2008]

MICHAIL MERSINIS

GRADUATED: GLASGOW SCHOOL OF ART
michaelmersinis@googlemail.com

It is the ambiguous representation of photography that provides a point of reference, and a genuine interest.

Especially the two invisible moments of the photographic process - image formation through light and light reacting with silver, The moment of the latent image is unique to photography and provides a space for questions that remain open.

Stripping all visible and recognizable aspects of the photographic image - reducing images to outlines on transparent surfaces, altering the appearance of spatial relationships by generating hybrids, returning virtual landscapes to silver are all inquiries regarding that moment after the exposure to the light.

When the silver starts to react and respond. When the latent image is formed. When all possibilities of the photographic representation are still undecided. When representation is not yet formed, the gesture of photography has not yet been made whole.

Before development and fixing, before the optical-chemical process is completed, the image is not yet set.

The result is not a statement, but an open question.

It is latent.

In that moment only the main primary elements of the image exist in a transient form.

Light and Silver.

Images from top:
Reclaimed Luminosity (Part V) [2008]
First Sea, Last Light [2008]

46

JANE MULVEY

GRADUATED: EDINBURGH COLLEGE OF ART, SCHOOL OF ARCHITECTURE

jane_mulvey@yahoo.co.uk

The Collective Incubator

Architecture operates as propaganda in this metaphoric representation of a city. Selected programmes act as vehicles to comment on banalisation while visitors are presented with new ways of thinking and better ways of living.

The Collective Incubator arose from examining the Scottish Central Belt. Neither rural or urban, the depressing sprawl offers no benefits. Designated urban strips will appear replacing the banality, which ultimately frees up surrounding land to be left natural, reinstated with forestry, and to introduce wind farms to generate a sustainable and self-sufficient future for the new cities.

With architecture comes the inherent responsibility of leaving a physical footprint. By responding to today's climate change (political, environmental, social and cultural), projects can embed these critical issues and become more than a space to inhabit, but a source for propaganda and a testing ground for new ideals and future living.

I experimented with this in my honours project, and continue to explore the potential further within my diploma topic of *Twenty-First Century Decadence*, which I am currently undertaking at the Royal Danish Academy of Fine Arts, Copenhagen. By tackling issues that some may avoid or find distressing, I intend not to force these ideas upon people, but display them so that a level of critical awareness and education into the subject matter can be achieved.

Whilst studying architecture, I have worked within the offices of Studio Daniel Libeskind in New York, and the Office for Metropolitan Architecture, Rotterdam. Both inspired and motivated me to a new destination in rigorous research and original thinking within architecture.

Images from top:
The Collective Incubator (Degree Show) [2008]
The Collective Incubator (Concept Model) [2008]

ASHLEY NIEUWENHUIZEN

GRADUATED: DUNCAN OF JORDANSTONE COLLEGE OF ART
www.myspace.com/morphbody

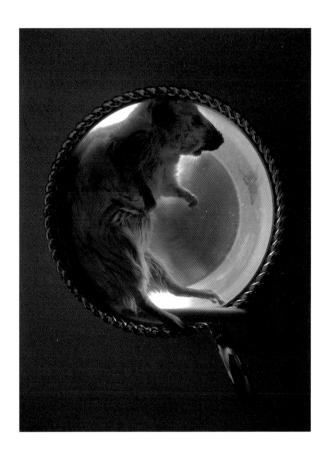

Inspired by the relationship, similarities and characteristics that animal and man share, my work portrays the realities of hybridization, domestication and animal industries, such as selective breeding programmes and battery farming. Using a variety of both repulsive and alluring materials in this body of work, from rabbit fur and pig nipples, to domestic objects and metal casts, I seek to create an environment that explores the realms within both human and animal kingdoms that affect the viewer's conscious and physical awareness. Ritual, sound and shamanistic ideas play a vital role in my practice, often depicting the physical and mental state of the artist, seen in my video performances and wearable sculptures. These ideas are found throughout the installation of my work, where one suggestion can be followed by another. This is demonstrated in the arrangement of particular complimentary and opposing pieces; wings sweeping from under a wooden table; appear to carry the shining white rodent, with bronze crows in a tangled tow, morphing from one 'idea' to another. Creating such dialogue between different pieces is imperative for the work to generate an environment, or united kingdom of both humans and animals, and to converse with the viewer's own physical and psychological self.

"...They have come from the unknown and bestowed the earth with magical kingdoms. I know these particular membranes are devouring as a miraculous harvest."

Nest [2008]

MICHAEL OWEN

GRADUATED: EDINBURGH COLLEGE OF ART

www.michaeljowen.co.uk

My practice is an exploration of form and material. I am particularly interested in man's relationship with environment. My work is a dialogue between 'the natural' and 'the man-made'. The process of working is extremely important to the content of my work. Whereas I am concerned about the final outcome of the work, I think the steps that lead to the end product is of great significance. A lot of my work is on found surfaces. I like the idea of salvaging and reshaping different surfaces as these materials can inject a literal aspect of the environment into my paintings. I am very interested in context of art and enjoy developing ideas outside the studio. I think this is an important aspect of my practice, where I explore a range of environments. The cube is a recurring image in my work. As I like to work quite spontaneously, the box forms keep some logic and structure in quite chaotic works. Scale is very important in my practice. I like moving between small drawings and large paintings, as it constantly changes the qualities between the two mediums. I mainly use black and white so I can fully concentrate on the structure of the works. This can give the work a precise analytical sense which can become quite architectural. I have recently toured the Far East, and feel this culture has influenced me. I also feel the works of Pedro Cabrita Reis, Isaac Monteiro, Lee Krasner and Franz Kline have inspired my practice.

Untitled [2008]

ROSS PERKIN

GRADUATED: UNIVERSITY OF EDINBURGH, SCHOOL OF ARCHITECTURE
rossperkin@gmail.com

The 2 year Master of Architecture (MArch) at the University of Edinburgh is an ambitious Part 2 course that seeks to integrate research and design in the production of architectural proposals for a specified European city. Over the course of academic year 2007-08, Ross developed a project for a Centre for Film in Andalucía within a decaying urban area of the dense historic fabric of the old town of Cádiz, on the Atlantic coast of south western Spain. Early fieldwork, historical and technological research led to meticulous documentation of this part of the city, and the site became understood as a shifting ground latent with the material remains of a Roman Circus. Ideas about porosity, typologies of entrances, the potency of the subterranean, excavation and the cultural role of spectacle have informed an urban strategy which literally and metaphorically reinforces the urban fabric. The architectural strategy is to precisely insert programmatic elements of El Ciné de las Torres which are held in mutual dependency while acting as support for the existing urban blocks. The new configuration of the cleared semi-public space is activated by film projection and public route. The material and spatial arrangement and language of the architectural proposal is inventive and develops a rich dialogue concerning weight, temporality and use.

Images from top:
El Ciné de las Torres: New Worlds within the Old Town of Cádiz [2008]
El Ciné de las Torres (detail) [2008]

GEORGINA PORTEOUS

GRADUATED: MORAY COLLEGE OF ART

Georginacp@aol.com

In my work I use a combination of found objects, automatic drawing and writing. Some of my objects are familiar yet taking them out of their context can render them unrecognisable. Their purpose can be questioned. The viewers are then at liberty to engage with the pieces, interpreting them in their own way, influenced by personal experience, emotion and attitude. Each individual will have a unique response. I see myself as a spatial artist using mixed media. My recent installations have made use of numerous materials including sound, video, bedpans and helium filled inflatables, snow globes, CAD designed squirrel embryos, formaldehyde and vaginal specula. I have been influenced by many artists but in particular Douglas Gordon, Jim Lambie, Pippilotti Rist, Mona Hatoum, Louise Bourgeois, Carsten Holler, Yayoi Kusama and Susan Collis.

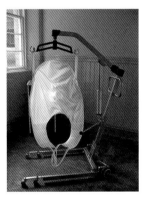
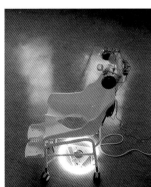

Images clockwise from top:
Fountainesque Tunnel into the Underbelly World (details) [2008]
Inflatable Foetus, Commode with sound installation, Hoist & Sling with film projection

MARY RAMSDEN

GRADUATED: EDINBURGH COLLEGE OF ART

mary.atticsalt@hotmail.com

Every aspect of my current practice is a component of a larger ongoing investigation. Through painting and text I attempt to manipulate the viewer's preconceptions of abstraction.

I am working with the archival material of Walter Benjamin and in particular the logged translations of his son's infantile linguistic formulations. I have created a systematic format for a further visual translation of this child's nonsensical language and annotated each phrase with a painting. These works are primarily about paint as a child's verbal distortions are about sound.

Benjamin entitled this period of investigation 'thoughts and opinions' ironically lending intellectual weight to these whimsical musings. As I associate each piece with a meaningless word I hope to challenge the treatment of 'the title'. This interplay with the observer induces an almost Sisyphean discourse primarily focusing on the intellectualisation of the abstract.

Mummerehlen (Series of 78 paintings) [2008]

DAISY RICHARDSON

GRADUATED: EDINBURGH COLLEGE OF ART

www.daisyrichardson.co.uk

The architectural interiors experienced in everyday life are deconstructed and fragmented. The features of our surroundings that would ordinarily be overlooked provide the inspiration for a very personal response in the form of a distinctive visual language. The smudges left behind by dripping condensation from a window, radiators and door furniture, all inspire the types of marks made. I have created a personal aesthetic which celebrates the subtleties of line and surface made possible through combining printmaking techniques. Through working in this manner, a range of marks and shapes have evolved into a descriptive and symbolic visual language. Although highly abstracted and personal this language describes everyday interiors. My preferred techniques are Etching and Stone Lithography. I enjoy combining several techniques to create rich, layered images which rejoice in the virtues of ink and paper. By working in print I am able to use the same image several times, combining it with different images, marks and papers to build varied compositions from the same building blocks. In this way the same marks appear again in a new guise somewhere else within a series. Like a written language it is repetitive and descriptive. Each image, like the words in a sentence, informs and relates to the rest of a series. They are in conversation. The full meaning of a series of prints is only fully realised when it is viewed as an entirety.

Smudge [2008]

GEMMA SAVILLE

GRADUATED: EDINBURGH COLLEGE OF ART
gemmasaville.blogspot.com

Synthesising the domestic environment with the natural, my practice considers both of their constructed ideals. Combining scientific and romantic approaches, I am currently exploring the possibilities inherent in scale, confusing the enormity of the natural with the relative modesty of the domestic.

In the realm of these environments, my work attempts to question the desire for possession, making solid souvenirs of imagined space. Stemming from an interest in the process of making, my current practice equally concerns retaining visual evidence of construction, creating a dialogue between the natural and the artifice from within the works themselves. The specific choice of materials and colours is vital to my work, and materials such as enamel paint, planed oak and hand coloured wax are employed to create compositions that appeal to our sensory capacities.

The installation of the objects and images creates varying sculptural combinations in which propped, leant and hung objects combine with photographic and drawn images, questioning the durational potential of sculpture. I want to suggest and explore the existence of a continuous narrative that appears to be unfolding in front of the viewer. Sculptural objects and images take on the powerful scale of the natural environment, but contained within the domestic space of the gallery, question its function.

Untitled (Wax Mountain) [2008]

54

TERESA SCIBERRAS

GRADUATED: GRAY'S SCHOOL OF ART

teresa.sciberras@gmail.com

My current work is fuelled by an ongoing interest in Medieval and early Renaissance art and iconography, and in part inspired by my recent trip to Florence on the Kinross scholarship.

Very often my paintings have a very personal starting point, though just as often they end up in the same place. This common ground is a concern with the ways in which, collectively and individually, we need to construct boundaries, to define inside from outside, known from unknown, self from other.

A recurring motif in my work has become that of the walled city, with its double-edged connotations of protection and confinement, security and threat, insularity and exile. Drawing on Derrida's ideas of the pharmakos (scapegoat), I find myself intrigued by the permeability of these structures and the potential for deconstruction which is always already there.

In short, what I attempt to allude to in my paintings is this process of construction, deconstruction and reconstruction - and the siege, the sacrifice and the burning which accompany it.

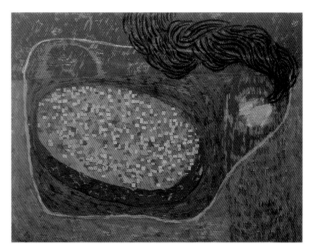

Images from top:
Pyrrhic Victory [2008]
The Library of Babel [2008]

HELEN SHADDOCK

GRADUATED: GLASGOW SCHOOL OF ART
www.helenshaddock.com

A scattering of words are connected by colour coded threads to form an expansive web that may, to one, appear as a confused mass of information, but are, to me, an organised diagram depicting a logical maze of elements that intertwine to characterise my practice.

Similarly, the basic actions that are taken to an extreme within my work could be interpreted as being apparently pointless, although the level of commitment to the given task suggests there is a motive that drives the behaviour.

My work stems from a fascination and visual attraction to organised information, lines, stripes, colour and repeated patterns. Order and chaos constantly challenge each other, and unexpected results emerge from highly controlled, obsessive and rigorous processes.

I enjoy the handmade aesthetic, where human elements are visible, and make reference to the everyday through the use of mundane materials.

Working with a range of media within pictorial and sculptural conventions, I engage the viewer both visually and experientially. The work becomes animated through my choice of material, and the playful and energetic nature introduces an element of humour. Constant change, movement, morphing, shifts in pace, and the manipulation of duration all act as devices to lure the viewer and prolong their engagement with the work. The installation of work brings together the various qualities within it, and allows me to play with the space of the viewer.

Kindly supported by Glasgow Visual Arts Grant Scheme.

Images from top:
Abacus [2008]
Weave [2008]

AISLING SHANNON

GRADUATED: SCOTT SUTHERLAND SCHOOL OF ARCHITECTURE

aisling_shannon@hotmail.com

The project brief called for the design of a hotel on a sloping site of great distinctiveness close to the Esplanade of the Historic Castle in Stirling.

Aisling developed her own brief for the site after undertaking a scholarly review of the context, place and nature of how we should make a building on such a site. Led by a deep rooted understanding of culture and history she proposes a design which learns from - and for - the site, blending new with old while reinforcing the eternal qualities of the place.

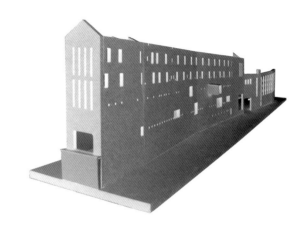

The design encompasses key moments in external and internal space that evoke memory and familiarity through proportion, atmosphere and tectonic expression. The outwardly cool and measured design response belies a depth and complexity of ideas that are revealed from formality to intimacy from the macro to the micro, in the site planning and linear expression of the 'inhabited wall', circulation and habitation patterns, the disposition of public and private space to the design of rooms, intimate places and thresholds. This 'meaningful' response is enforced with a knowledge and attention detail of how things are made.

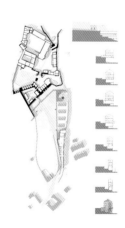

"This boutique hotel sits within a wall at Stirling Castle. Thick concrete walls contain niches which offer intimate moments, and a sense of ownership. The design is solid and monolithic like the castle walls, becoming small-scale and vernacular to relate with the neighbouring old town buildings. The view is an event, not a constant. In-situ concrete walls are cast against textured wallpaper internally, offering a luxurious, tactile finish. The hotel seeks to improve a visitor's experience of the Castle; the Esplanade, currently a car park, becomes a civic gathering space, contributing to a sense of arrival at Castle and hilltop." Aisling Shannon.

Images from top:
A Hotel Within a Wall at Stirling Castle [2008]

BRIDGET STEED

GRADUATED: EDINBURGH COLLEGE OF ART
www.bridgetsteed.co.uk

My work uncovers the different pasts and connections of a site, recording and documenting their identities, inhabitants and situation and creating reminders to these lost places and their histories.

From the recent site of a grand Edinburgh property at 37 Inverleith Place, my work has been taken to the remote location of Leith Harbour on South Georgia, Antarctica, and with a Scottish Arts Trust bursary, I will travel there in October 2009 to spend three months working in the Grytviken whaling museum. These two derelict and abandoned places come together in my work, connected through a past resident, whaling fleet owner Theodore Salvesen. Exploring their shared histories, these allied but distant sites are brought together, where their pasts and imagery are combined and my experience of them is recorded. Each chapter of their pasts has left visible traces and through a combination of documentation, detailed research and invented relics I have created a narrative that exposes the stories of these places and illustrated their visual connections.

Images from top:
Antarctic Circle [2008]
Scrimshaw [2008]

STEPHANIE STRAINE

GRADUATED: EDINBURGH COLLEGE OF ART

stephanie.straine@googlemail.com

The lens is a geometrically generated, industrially produced object, which, in its strikingly simple appearance, masks an incredible complexity.

Looking: detached from the necessity of an external referent or focal point. The pure mechanics of perception.

The subject is removed, leaving only the condition of the edge: that uncertain territory of vision, which exposes its discontinuous, imperfect nature. The surface is marked with physical traces simultaneously abstract and indexical. Drawing becomes a liminal space, where concrete information slips into ambiguity.

A tension between structure and provisionality.

A sliver of space between haptics and optics.

The grinding of a progressive surface involves the plotting of almost 50,000 data points into a numerically controlled grinding machine. The starting point of the grinding process is the centre of the lens. The combination of movement along x and y directions and simultaneous rotations forms a spiral pattern on the lens.

The meeting of the grid and the circle, or part-circle: curve, parabola, and edge.

The insistence of two surfaces forced together; the pressure, both direct and indirect, of this mechanised touch.

Correcting something by permitting something else to disappear.

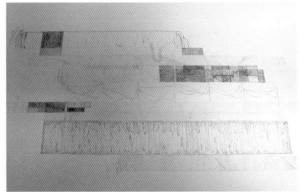

Images from top:
Variable Set (detail) [2008]
Lantal 1.5 [2008]

CAMILLA SYMONS

GRADUATED: DUNCAN OF JORDANSTONE COLLEGE OF ART
www.camillasymons.co.uk

The subject matter of my silverpoint drawings relates to discoveries of life and death in nature from my youth: the myxomatosis rabbit, dead birdling and the crow with the broken wing.

The work recognises these childhood rites of passage. It is an adult understanding of the underlying themes of morality, origin and mortality that I witnessed as a child. The silverpoint takes time, slowly building up layers and marks and monumentalises the gritty, damp fur and feathers of the characters that have remained in my mind throughout my life. In time the silverpoint alters in colour and depth.

With all of my work I aim to achieve something beautiful and whimsical but tainted with a sad, unnerving quality.

Fur of the Outcast 2 (detail) [2008]

EUAN TAYLOR

GRADUATED: DUNCAN OF JORDANSTONE COLLEGE OF ART

inefficientsolutions@googlemail.com

As Chief Director of Inefficient Solutions I oversee all operations. I ensure that Inefficient Solutions strives to deliver the best in all our specialized areas which include:

Creating and Solving Problems

Purveyors of Superficial Commodities

Digging a way out the Hole

Futile Endeavour

Currently working as a sub-contractor for Ganghut. A new avenue of pursuit has arisen which Inefficient Solutions intends to exploit to and beyond its full potential. When promise of a rich source of wealth reached the Ganghut construction site, Inefficient Solutions was quick to diversify its core operations. The north east of Scotland has a long established relationship with working the land, utilizing natural resources through machinery. Through sophisticated research, Inefficient Solutions now knows what this machinery looks like and so is ready to begin formulating a plan ensuring stability in uncertain times.

Cloud Muncher (sketch) [2008]

ROBIN THOMSON

GRADUATED: DUNCAN OF JORDANSTONE COLLEGE OF ART
www.robinthomsononline.com

Whether it's a mechanical sculpture, photograph or a narrative video, the essence of the work is one of exploration and experimentation: reviewing the means by which we 'look beyond' our everyday environments. I liken the process of working as a way of orienting myself within the world. These exploratory studies into our everyday environment sometimes take on the role of pseudo-scientific investigation. Narratives are implicitly 'written' into objects, where the processes, appropriations and re-presentation might be considered as forming a structural narrative. Exploring these objects as 'vehicles', I evaluate their ability to carry ideas and watch how they lose or develop new meanings along the way. The art making overlooks the gathering up of those pieces left in the space between symbols and their interpretation: an expanse wherein meanings are constructed and conveyed, resembling something like artefacts from a faraway culture. I am interested in reversing the static nature of things around me, in particular mass produced products opposing the crafted and unique object. Through common media – newspapers, household appliances and furniture– I try to make something that transcends it's commonality at the same time as using the materials that embody it, like trying to break through rational language with a highly personal voice; at the same time surrendering to its logic. The end products are like the uncanny souvenirs brought back from travels into the realm of a manufactured subjectivity: an actual 'journey' through the realms of creativity, leaving the detritus of the imagination strewn along the path.

Images from top:
Corner of the Universe (Installation) [2008]
Sledge [2007]

ROSIE WALTERS

GRADUATED: EDINBURGH COLLEGE OF ART

www.rosie-walters.com

Through the practice of drawing I invent portals for adventure. This theme evolves from a fascination with creating alternative and fictitious spaces and contraptions - transportation devices are contrived, vertical cities are constructed and imagined landscapes are portrayed. Visual inspiration comes from real 'things' and spaces - wandering in scrap yards, car boot sales, museums and cities; rummaging through libraries and dusty shelves; and dissecting old pieces of machinery. Each opens a multitude of possibilities to seek out, explore and adventure into alternative worlds. With this archive of images, objects and words I piece together my own spaces for exploration. Improvisation during the process of drawing is key to my practice as it allows continuous invention. In this way I am able to explore the potential of the line and its ability, when pieced together, to create fictitious spaces.

Diver's Escape [2008]

63

RIC WARREN

GRADUATED: GLASGOW SCHOOL OF ART

www.ricwarren.blogspot.com

I am interested in the changes of our built environment (physically, politically, culturally and environmentally) and I repeatedly attempt to hypothesise potential conclusions of such adjustments to our habitat. I find inspiration from the structures and materials that compose our manmade surroundings and I am particularly interested in architecture. My work primarily manifests itself in the form of sculptural installations, yet I consider drawing as an equally important aspect of my creative practice and process. Spaces that are visually concealed or made physically inaccessible intrigue me and I try to explore these concerns within my work. My structures and models attempt to mimic the language of architecture, or intervene with it, to create buildings that hold space, but do not offer it. Similarly, my drawings take the guise of working engineering drawings, yet are intentionally flawed to render them void of their supposed "function".

Neighbourhood Watch [2008]

REBECCA WITKO

GRADUATED: EDINBURGH COLLEGE OF ART

www.noise.net/rebeccawitko

The key elements of my work are line, shape and colour. I explore the relationship between these elements within my compositions creating bold, colourful statements. There is a graphic element to my work which is created through linear drawing.

My compositions are translations and reconstructions of my surrounding environment. I take elements from my research and manipulate them playing with scale, colour and shape in order to reconstruct my own interpretation of an environment.

The incorporation of an element that can be moved in the structures that have become my work creates a new dynamic, allowing the image to change slightly altering what is initially presented to the viewer and introducing a playful side to my practice.

My research comprises of photographs of urban environments, ranging from industrial scenes to modern architecture. From them I create drawings, which can be used as works on their own or manipulated to produce a variety of installations. I have developed towards assembling and constructing, using multiple pieces to create a dynamic image. I make these structures by layering and building away from the canvas.

I try to create as little association to my research material in my pieces as possible leaving them very open for the viewer's personal interpretation whatever that maybe. I overwhelm the viewer with compositions that are full of visual information that should stimulate a pleasing reaction.

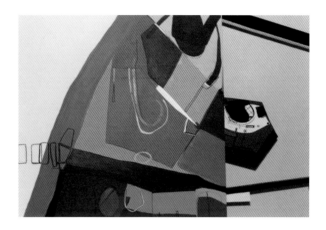

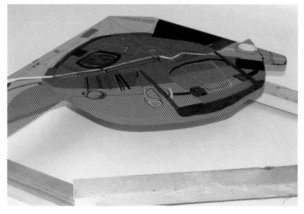

Wooden Structure Installation (details) [2008]

JULIE WYNESS

GRADUATED: GRAY'S SCHOOL OF ART
julie@forseat.demon.co.uk

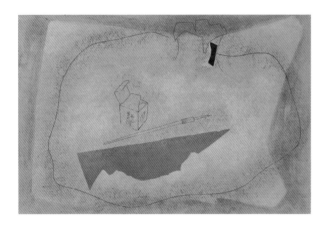

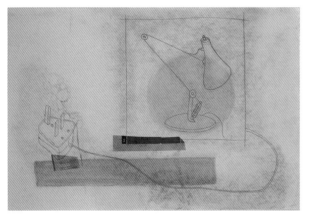

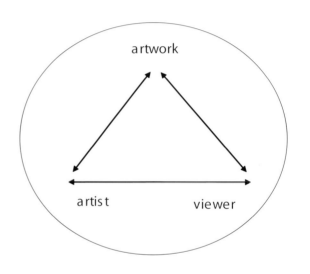

Images from top:
Pomegranate with Pink [2009]
Lamp with Yellow [2009]

RSA NEW CONTEMPORARIES

RSA Sir William Gillies Bequest Award [£2000]
RSA Painting Prize & the Maclaine Watters Medal [£400]
RSA Sculpture Prize [£400]
RSA Architecture Prize [£400]
RSA Printmaking Prize [£400]
RSA Carnegie Travelling Scholarship [£200]
RSA Adam Bruce Thomson Award [£100]
RSA Landscape Award [£100]
RSA Chalmers Bursary [£75]
RSA Stuart Prize [£50]
RSA Chalmers-Jervise Prize [£30]

The Stevenston Award for Painting [£5000]
Hope Scott Trust Postgraduate Award [£1000]
Friends of the Royal Scottish Academy Award [£500]
Standard Life Investments Property Investment Architecture Award [£500]

Peacock Visual Arts Award for Moving Image
6 months free access to Peacock's digital facility

Edinburgh Printmakers Award
Printmaking course, membership and a studio sessions

Edinburgh Sculpture Workshop Graduate Research Award
One month working in one of the ESW garden Pavilions plus fee, support and free membership

The Skinny Award
Exhibition opportunity, online/magazine editorial and associated publicity

Rendezvous Gallery/Linda Clark Nolan Award
Painting residency in Lewis and invitiation to take part in the Gaelic Connections exhibition at Rendezvous Gallery during 2009

Scotland's Colleges Award
Awarded to artists who have studied at a Scottish FE College prior to their current course

David Gordon Memorial Trust Awards
For works by artists born or studying in Grampian Region

ACKNOWLEDGEMENTS

RSA NEW CONTEMPORARIES 2009

The Royal Scottish Academy would like to thank John McLaren for use of his image to publicise the exhibition. Thanks also to the Hanging Committee: Will Maclean RSA (Convener), Dick Cannon RSA (Elect), John Byrne RSA (Elect), Joyce W Cairns RSA, Thomas Joshua Cooper RSA (Elect), Sandy Moffat RSA (Elect), John Mooney RSA, Arthur Watson RSA, the Exhibition Staff and Neil Mackintosh and his team for their work in presenting the show. Also thanks to the staff of the Art Colleges and Architecture Schools in Scotland for their invaluable input and support; Dr Joanna Soden and the Collections Team and Sheena Walker and the Friends of the RSA for their work on The RSA Friends of the RSA School Competition Exhibition 'Focus on Print'; Lara Moloney at The Skinny; Jane Nicol at Sheep Dip Malt Whisky; and to Lynn Haxton and Stewarts of Edinburgh for their invaluable assistance in delivering the catalogue.

Also thanks to the prize-givers: The Stevenston Trust; The Hope-Scott Trust; The Friends of the RSA; Standard Life Property Investment; Rendezvous Gallery; Linda Clark Nolan; Scotland's Colleges; The David Gordon Memorial Trust; Peacock Visual Arts; Edinburgh Sculpture Workshop; Edinburgh Printmakers Workshop; and The Skinny.

We wish to extend a very special thanks to our media partner The Skinny and our print partner Stewarts of Edinburgh.

Administration by Colin R Greenslade, Pauline Costigane, Alisa Lindsay, Susan Junge, Gail Gray and Kirsty Dickson.
Exhibition Staff: Daniel Goodwin, Lucinda Greig, Brian Hewitt, Caroline Lambie, Thom Laycock, Shona Macnaughton, Lindsey Michie, Emma Pratt, Olga Rek, Jamie Robinson, Cosima Sempill, Christine Shuker, Bridget Steed, Derek Sutherland

Catalogue designed and typeset by Alisa Lindsay
Printed by Stewarts of Edinburgh

Published in the United Kingdom by the Royal Scottish Academy of Art & Architecture
for the exhibition RSA New Contemporaries, 14 - 25 February 2009
The Royal Scottish Academy of Art & Architecture
The Mound, Edininbrugh, EH2 2EL

ISBN 978 0 905783 178